BACKLESS BETTY FROM BONDI

Other light verse by Kenneth Slessor
available from ETT Imprint

DARLINGHURST NIGHTS

BACKLESS BETTY FROM BONDI

KENNETH SLESSOR

illustrated by
VIRGIL REILLY,
FRANK DUNNE and
JOAN MORRISON

edited by Julian Croft

First paperback edition published by ETT Imprint 2020

ETT IMPRINT
PO Box R1906
Royal Exchange NSW 1225
Australia

First published by Angus & Robertson 1983
First electronic edition published by ETT Imprint 2020

ISBN 978-1-922473-02-8 pbk
ISBN 978-1-922473-03-5 ebk

The author is grateful to Smith's Weekly, who first
published these verses and drawings in their newspaper.

INTRODUCTION

In 1926 Kenneth Slessor returned to Sydney after a brief period working on Melbourne newspapers. Fellow poet Robert D. FitzGerald was surprised to see him walking down Martin Place with a bag of golf clubs over his shoulder (Slessor had never played golf), and even more surprised when Slessor told him that he was going to give up writing poetry of the kind he had been writing, and to concentrate only on humorous poetry. FitzGerald did not take him seriously. But Slessor was in earnest. His manuscripts and rhyming dictionaries in the National Library in Canberra show how seriously he took the task of writing light verse. The manuscripts reveal piles of rhymes stacked like roulette chips, and lists of brand names, foods, clothing, in unlikely but rhyming combination. Betty Riddell remembers him in his lunch hour, fingers bloodied with beetroot sandwiches, carefully writing his verses for *Smith's Weekly*, the satirical paper which he joined in 1927 and where he was to work for the next twelve years.

In February of 1928, the first of Slessor's light verse illustrated by Virgil Reilly ("As We Pine in a Line") appeared. More than seventy-five pieces (most of them illustrated by Virgil, others by Frank Dunne and Joan Morrison) were to come out in *Smith's Weekly* over the next ten years. As well as writing a sizeable proportion of the paper's copy, visiting the "pagoda of pugdom" to fill in for the boxing writer, reviewing films and books and later acting as editor, Slessor found time to write his elegant and witty observations of life in Sydney before and during the Depression.

Forty-two of the Slessor/Virgil collaborations were published in 1933 in a collection called *Darlinghurst Nights*. Reprinted in 1981, it consists of verse written and illustrated between 1928 and 1931. The present collection reprints those verses not previously collected and covers the period February 1928 to November 1933.

As in *Darlinghurst Nights*, it is possible to see in these poems the darker side of the Depression and to see in some of them hints of the melancholy which develops in Slessor's serious poetry in the thirties. But in the main they are light in touch, even when they deal with subjects dear to the editorial heart of *Smith's*: the returned serviceman, censorious wowsers, the battler during the Depression. Where the verse shines is in the enjoyment of living. The inheritance of Norman Lindsay can still be seen; but Virgil has slimmed down his models and dressed them in Chanel, and Slessor has opted for the less idealised women of Lindsay's novels rather than the fantasies of his paintings and engravings.

It is a world of externals: clothing, motor cars, yachts, aeroplanes, the tatty and the fashionable, not the world of metaphysics and unattainable beauty. Was it a result of the Depression, or a turning away from the inflated seriousness of Modernism? Whatever, Romance in 1930 was a way out of the spiritual depressions of the Slump, a cheap escape from the cruel fiscal realities preached by Sir Otto Niemeyer, and a way of enjoying the senses free from the control of the state or the economy:

> *The sky is still with magic blent,*
> *The heart still cries a tune —*
> *Who'll cut the night by Ten Per Cent.,*
> *And who can tax the moon?*
>
> *A tram is cheap, a kiss is free,*
> *Whate'er the bank proposes;*
> *We'll swap your Otto L.S.D.*
> *For Otto made from roses!*
> ("Night of Romance")

Have the poems faded? I don't think so, and that is not because the economic cycle has just completed another fifty-year turn and we can sense an uncanny correspondence with things as they were in 1932. More importantly, the poems in this collection show us that poetry can be entertaining, witty, verbally inventive and still make a point fifty years later. What has been fading in the poetry of the last two decades are these very qualities, and perhaps through the fun and enjoyment of light verse, poetry might free itself from some of the worst excesses of the ego and look at the world again through a set of alive senses. *Plus ça change*: backless Betty is now topless Betty, but Bondi and its freedom and its hedonists can be examples for us all in time of Depression:

> *Oh, make the great Pacific dry,*
> *And drive the council speechless,*
> *Remove the breakers from Bondi —*
> *The beach, and leave us beachless,*
> *The fair, the bare, the naked-backed,*
> *The beer, the pier, the jetty —*
> *TAKE ANYTHING AT ALL, IN FACT,*
> *BUT LEAVE, OH LEAVE US BETTY!*

Julian Croft

CONTENTS

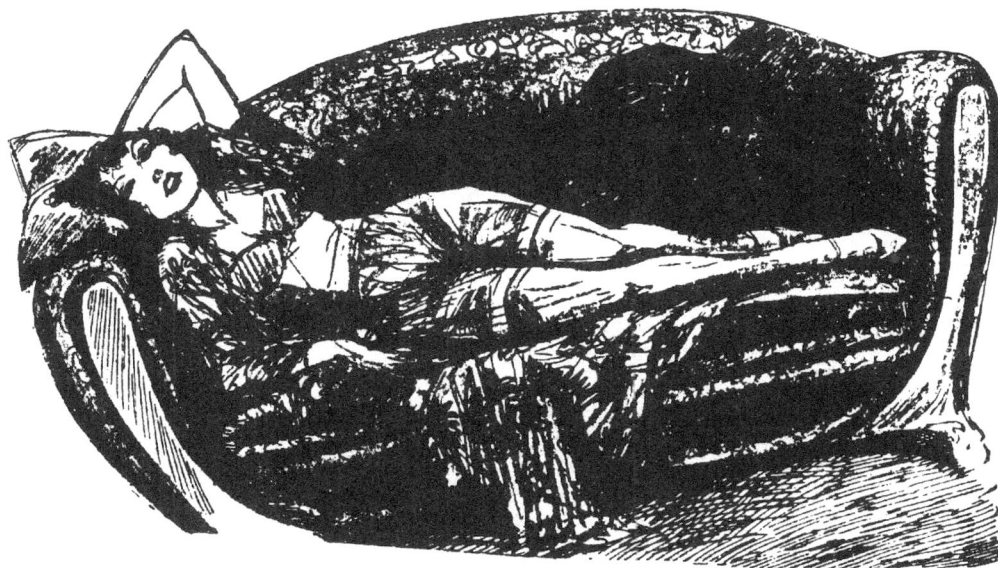

BACKLESS BETTY FROM BONDI

The Man Who Came Back

"Smith's" has received a letter from Papakura, Auckland (N.Z.), as follows: "Circumstances prevented me from getting my 'Smith's' since last March. The last one I had, Oigle had grown up. I have now got a job, and am getting 'Smith's' again... It is difficult to explain how you miss 'Smith's'... The paper never lost its brightness in our time of trouble ..."

"*You can wander the streets without weeping,*
Do without butter on bread,
Blankets aren't needed for sleeping,
Beer only goes to your head,
Pinching a belt with a buckle
Is only a kind of a knack —
But fighting bare-knuckle with never a chuckle
Is Hell!"
Said the Man Who Came Back.

"*When you choke in the bogs of dejection*
Up to your sorrowful chin,
Stiff at the end of the section,
That's when you ache for a grin;
That's when you wail at the winter,
Hearing the icicles crack;
But let 'em all splinter — thank God for a printer
And 4d
To bring the sun back!

"*All you far-away men in the city*
Jesting with Indian ink,
Drawing me jokes out of pity,
Pause for a moment and think —
What do I care about money?
Blankets and butter may lack,
But life is still sunny as long as YOU'RE funny —
KEEP ON!"
Said the Man Who Came Back.

NIGHT OF ROMANCE

Let Banks and Bailiffs rule the land —
  Oh, what do lovers care?
The tide still floats upon the sand,
  The moon still rules the air.

The sky is still with magic blent,
  The heart still cries a tune —
Who'll cut the night by Ten Per Cent.,
  And who can tax the moon?

A tram is cheap, a kiss is free,
  Whate'er the bank proposes;
We'll swap your Otto L.S.D.
  For Otto made from roses!

Mademoiselle from Everywhere

(To the Digger — Memories)

The girl that you kissed at Putney,
  O, what is she doing to-day?
She's married to Somebody's chutney
  And living out Beckenham way.
You called her your daffodil fairy
  (She threw you a flower on a punt),
But those were the days, O, the magical days,
  When the real Tipperary
  Was far from the Front.

And you have gone over the water —
  Behold, you've an office and phone! —
And she has a grown-up daughter
  Who weighs about seventeen stone.
But sometimes a touch of the liver
  In suburbs where aldermen dwell,
Will bring back the days (ah, the far-away days!)
  When you kissed on the river
  A. W. L.

The girl that you kissed at Calais,
  Or pledged at Beersheba with beer,
Or danced with all night at a Palais,
  Or lied to all night on a pier,
Is older and staider and fatter,
  She's vanished with vanishing cream —
But those were the days, those miraculous days,
  And what does it matter,
  You've still got your dream!

In a life of brick bungs. and De Sotos
  And pansies — if such is your life —
You can turn out your postcards and photos,
  Retaining one eye on the wife.
She's gone with her daffodil kisses,
  She's floated away into air,
And, oh, the old days, the incredible days,
  Are what SHE never misses
  And YOU never dare!

NOCTURNE

"The Daily Telegraph Pictorial" and the "Sun" have been printing vile slurs on our Australian girlhood — allowing them to be called, without exception, "clandestine prostitutes".

Darkness; a cloud of lace;
  Shines in the quiet air
Barbara's pale and lovely face
  In a rain of yellow hair.
Moonlight smoking below...
  Barbara lazily blinks —
Barbara, evening papers know,
  Is a shameless minx.

Smear her! Slime her!
  Cover her with scum!
Shrilly from the toadstools
  the little voices hum.

Night like a golden dust
  Trembles upon the trees;
Caught in a strayed September gust,
  Marjory hugs her knees.
Silence across the bay...
  Only the cry of a gull...
Marjory, evening papers say,
  Is a brazen trull.

Daub her! Foul her!
  Dirty her with mud!
Shrilly from the quagmire
  the little voices flood.

Under a sleeping tree,
  Water and stars and night,
Dorothy looks at the running sea;
  Eyes that are crystal bright;
Fingers that fairies kiss,
  Powder and puff to dab —
Dorothy, evening papers hiss,
  Is a heartless drab.

Smirch her! Soil her!
  Drag her in the gutter!
Shrilly from the midden
  the little voices mutter.

The GIRL at the GATE

Out of the bush behind her,
     You come in your scornful car;
There on the gate you'll find her,
     Locking for Lochinvar.
But sentiment rarely rankles,
     And nobody wishes to wait,
When she dances on little brown ankles
     To open —
               how very obliging! —
     To open the Nine Mile Gate.

Open and shut, open and shut —
     Lochinvar scorns to wait.
He's vanished, alas, in a cloud of gas,
Poor little Girl at the Gate!

Cars that go past in thunder,
     How can they understand?
Open the gate, and wonder —
     Close it, and wave your hand.
Can you pin your heart to a placard,
     Or wish that he struck you dead,
When a Prince in a fairy Packard
     Throws you a coin —
               how generous! —
     Throws you a coin instead?

Open and shut, open and shut,
     Nobody wants to wait,
You're a speck on the track, and they never look back,
     Poor little Girl at the Gate.

FIREFLY

Dedicated to the usherettes of the picture
palaces of Australia and their torchlights.

I've fallen in love with a firefly,
  Two legs and a flambeau complete,
A heavenly smile as she runs down the aisle,
  And a laugh as she bangs down the seat.

Don't tell me she lives at Clovelly,
  Don't say that she catches a tram,
Or dotes on "Vendetta" by Marie Corelli,
  And loves to eat pickles and ham.
She comes as a comet to Halley,
  Assisting a duke to his place —
A cloud of gold fire, like a star in the valley,
  Two legs and a dim, little face.
I don't adore Mae or Dolores,
  Or give Greta Garbo my heart,
Nor yet the particular glories
  American pictures impart.
The statues can rust in a thicket,
  The Wurlitzer gives me a pain;
If it wasn't a firefly who gazed on my ticket,
  I wouldn't have come here again.

And I know when I go to St. Peter,
  He'll call out his staff with a grin —
A Devil, no doubt, to show the Way Out,
  But a firefly to light the Way In!

AS WE PINE IN A LINE

Half-an-inch, half-an-inch, lumbering near,
  Over the landscape and down to the punt,
Austins are squealing with rage in the rear,
  Packards are roaring in front;
Buicks are braying, Hupmobiles neighing,
Sirens are playing, toot, toot;
Horace and Doris, asleep in their Morris —
Frankly they don't give a hoot,
      WHILE,
With many a grumble and grunt,
We slumber and shuffle and shunt,
We rattle and curse like a slow-motion hearse,
      As we pine
          in
          a
          line
          for
          the
          PUNT.

Oh, well for the rollicking medico's boy,
  Dashing so carelessly down to the front.
Well for the bicyclist, beaming with joy,
  Bouncing his bike on the punt;
The doctor's pal cadges his B.M.A. badges
For Maudies and Madges en route,
And girls riding pillion whizz past by the million,
In clouds of face powder, toot, toot!
      But,
One-eighth of an inch to the front,
We grumble and rumble and shunt,
We brood in a trance, or destroy the white ants,
      As we pine
          in
          a
          line
          for
          the
          PUNT.

COME ABOARD

When Someone in Yellow
  Comes over the side,
The officers bellow,
  The bo'suns collide.
The boilers can blister,
  The stokers don't care,
If Somebody's Sister
  Comes visiting there.

She's full of inquiries,
  Instruction she begs:
Do captains write diaries?
  And what are sea-legs?
And who is Blue Peter?
  And how many tons?
And isn't it neater
  To Duco the guns?

But nobody's able
  To fidget or frown,
With ''Really, Miss Mabel?''
  And ''Won't you sit down?''
And everyone's ''Mr.'',
  I'm glad to confide,
When Somebody's Sister
  Comes over the side.

The Admiral pauses,
  The sailors all sigh,
She probably causes
  The compass to lie —
And O, what a glister
  Of manners there'd be
If Somebody's Sister
  Were always at sea!

BUTTERFLIES

If anyone's looking for Mary,
  She's fallen in love with a star —
You'll have to employ a canary
  To go so impossibly far.
In vain do the cabarets thunder,
  In vain does the Burgundy froth,
She'll never be happy Down Under —
  A Butterfly up in a Moth.

The engine's too loud for entreaty,
  Your signals excite her disdain,
You'll have to produce a Wapiti,
  Or shout from a neighbouring 'plane.
She sneers at the heartbroken caller
  Who comes in a Marmon or Hup,
And Packards look very much smaller
  From Five Thousand Feet Farther Up!

No doubt she resembles a fairy —
  I always knew fairies could fly —
But I didn't expect to find Mary
  So very disturbingly high!

Permit me to borrow a Widgeon,
  Or climb up and wave from a bough,
Or bribe a compassionate pigeon —
  She's got her certificate now!

UNDERWOOD ANN"

(TO A SECRETARY)

Her fingers to sell,
  Her patience to loan,
A slave of the bell,
  She kneels by the throne;
You people who wait
  May pester and plan,
Your ultimate Fate
  Is Underwood Ann.

Underwood Ann,
  Underwood Ann,
She talks like a fairy and
  acts like a man;
The voice that arranges
  and chooses and changes,
It isn't the boss,
  but it's Underwood Ann.

You wait on the mat,
  She taps on her keys —
Don't frown about that,
  Sit down, if you please —
The will that you cross,
  The face that you scan,
It isn't the boss,
  It's Underwood Ann.

Underwood Ann,
  Underwood Ann,
You'd like to get past her,
  but nobody can;
It's easy to hector
  a common director,
But what about hectoring
  Underwood Ann?

One blink of her eye,
  The boss mutters "No";
He utters a sigh,
  She runs the whole show.
The smile that rewards,
  That blesses or bans,
It isn't the Board's,
  It's Underwood Ann's.

Underwood Ann,
  Underwood Ann;
Underwood, underworld,
  underclothes Ann,
Grimness and graces,
  Napoleon in laces,
General Manager
  Underwood Ann!

SKIS AND SKATES

I sing about Women and Winter,
  The rapture of 30 degrees,
The damsel who waits with a bundle of skates
  And the girl who goes riding on skis;
And, oh for the flight of an eagle
  To see where she happens to go —
But waving a wing is a difficult thing
  When you lie with your face in the snow.

Poo-pooh to your ice, Kosciusko,
  A fig for your cucumber air,
Your peaks, I'm informed, are sufficiently warmed
  By the presence of Annabel there;
But this I'm unable to warrant,
  The fact is, I really don't know —
Wherever I climb I spend most of my time
  With my face in a puddle of snow.

I know she has wings
  on her ankles,
I know she can
  leap like a trout,
The hoi-polloi thrill
  when she whistles downhill
And the guides find
  their eyes popping out;
For this I'll accept
  without question
The word of the
  Tourist Bureau —
My personal view
  is a trifle askew
Due to banging my
  face in the snow.

If only my skis wouldn't wobble,
  If only my feet would go straight,
I'd chase her with hope down a nursery slope
  And leave introductions to Fate;
But something has doomed me to grovel,
  I crawl on all fours down below,
She catapults by like a bird in the sky,
  And I lie with my face in the snow.

11

She Keeps on Walking

When Helen goes hiking
You'll have to provide
The heels of a Viking
To walk at her side;
At such a fierce canter
She chooses to tread,
Her blue tam-o'-shanter
Is always ahead.

You mumble and grumble,
She burns up the dust,
Her feet never stumble,
Her boots never bust;
With cramp in each muscle,
By moonlight you'll find,
In spite of all bustle,
You're mountains behind.

In haunts far and hilly
Where centipedes play,
She brings out a billy
To round off the day;
Disdainfully humming,
She waits for a man,
But nobody's coming,
For nobody can.

The knights of the dryad,
So deep their despair,
With harsh jeremiad
Embitter the air,
With groans beyond measure
They fall by the track —
SHE lolls at her leisure,
Her suitors walk back!

SHE SHOOTS TO CONQUER

When Kitty "shoots" to conquer,
   Like wings her ankles beat,
A golden whirl engulfs the girl
   And bubbles drown her feet.
A thousand waves attend her,
   With foam and passion quaking,
And the gulls ride on the warm tide
   Like a white flower breaking.

To brave the deepest breaker
   Or don the belt for Beauty,
The beach-patrols would sell their souls,
   As is, indeed, their duty.
But, mocked by hopeless fancy,
   They pine ashore, disputing;
And the sun burns and the tide turns
   And she keeps on shooting!

NIGHTINGALE — 1930

The music that warmed Asia Minor
When nightingales perched on the bough
Was certainly never diviner
Than nightingales give to us now.
In corridors dismal and dirty,
A Lady went forth with a Lamp —
To-day, Nineteen Hundred and Thirty,
It's Jones —
    Little Jones —
    Florence Nightingale Jones —
With Rontgen and radium, wireless and phones,
Who walks in the ward, 1930,
As Nightingale walked in the camp.

Her name is most probably Mary,
Though Sisters address her as "Jones" —
A kind of iodoform fairy,
The Board in its majesty owns.
She sets all the Fahrenheit foaming —
Behold our thermometer-charts —
And pulses go faster than Gloaming
When Jones —
    Mary Jones —
    The girl they call "Jones" —
With murder for microbes and magic for moans,
Down rows of white pillows goes roaming,
Severely affecting our hearts.

Oh, bring out your wogs in a wagon,
Wherever bacteria stir,
St. George and his twopenny dragon
Had nothing whatever on her.
She doesn't do much, but it's plenty;
She doesn't say much, but it sings —
And, Oh! the effect on Ward Twenty
When Jones —
    You know Jones —
    Probationer Jones —
A smile on her face and an ache in her bones,
Comes floating along to Ward Twenty,
This Nightingale minus the wings!

14

THE GIRL ON THE CORNER

Oh, what does she wait for,
  The girl over there,
And who could be late for
  A creature so fair?
Forlorn and forlorner,
  One eye on the clock,
She stands on a corner,
  Bewitching the block.

Who made the appointment,
  And what does he mean,
This fly in the ointment
  So late on the scene?
Displaying his label,
  She waits on the spot —
It must be CLARK GABLE
  Or someone like SCOTT!

She stands there, half-smiling,
  Half-biting her nails,
Completely beguiling
  An army of males;
Though someone forgot her
  For several hours,
The moment THEY spot her,
  They rush to buy flowers.

They plunder the florist's,
  They ogle and surge,
While scampering forests
  Of roses converge,
But deaf to each greeting
  And blind to each beam,
The girl No One's meeting
  Waits on in a dream.

Well, have a good snigger,
  Then ponder on this —
A little old figure
  Limps up with a kiss;
A smile and a chiding,
  A tram for the Quay —
Away they go riding
  To grandmother's tea!

LITTLE THEATRE GIRL

Oh, magic patch of Culture
  Where foreheads mount so high
They rise above the vulture
  And bid the skylark fly,
Your brows are not so dizzy
  But SHE can make them whirl —
That pretty little busy little
  Little Theatre Girl!

Not hers the sordid scramble
  Of dancing for a wage —
Like Mrs. Patrick Campbell
  She stalks another stage,
Where men of perfect breeding
  Do all the Walking On,
And all the parts are "leading",
  And all the cares have gone.

On plays by Pirandello
  She sprinkles sex-appeal,
And titbits from "Othello"
  And trifles by O'Neill.

The works of D. H. Lawrence
  She talks about all night —
In private with abhorrence,
  In public with delight.

What if she thinks that Strindberg
  Is just a kind of cheese,
Or mixes him with Lindbergh —
  Who cares for things like these?
We love her willy-nilly,
  We listen in a whirl —
That silly little frilly little
  Little
    Theatre
      Girl!

Streamer's End

Roses all over the steamer,
    Paper all over the sky,
And You at the end of a streamer
    Smiling goodbye, goodbye.
It isn't to me you dangle,
    It isn't to me you smile,
But out of the rainbow tangle
    Our lines have crossed for a while.

Somebody's benediction
    Pitches a streamer — whizz! —
Under the firm conviction
    You're on the end of his.
Others may claim attention,
    Rolling away to sea,
But nobody's there to mention
    The cove at this end is ME!

Don't you consider the danger
    Of setting a heart on fire
By tossing a perfect stranger
    Your 10,000 volt live-wire?
I'm only a face on the skyline,
    Something the wharf obscures —
But you're on the end of my line,
    And I'm on the end of yours!

Off in the vast Orsova,
    Soon you will wave in vain;
I could be Casanova,
    You could be Queen of Spain —
I must go back to the city,
    You must go back to the King.
Blow me a kiss for pity,
    Girl at the end of the string!

SPRING

Treetops crying, pipits in the creek,
Flowers go flying in a blackbird's beak,
Peach-boughs whirl, hens count eggs,
And a girl comes running like a flower on legs.

There she walks, where the cherry-boughs blow,
Lighting up their stalks with a sweet pink snow,
Strawberries to toss, lavender to fling,
This blue-eyed blossom by the name of Spring!

Spring with her fiddles and her fair, blue skies —
Ask no riddles and she'll tell no lies;
Take her at her word, kiss her when she comes,
Act like a bird and pick up crumbs!

Joy goes jigging — hey, for the guitar! —
Don't go digging underneath too far;
Down below the sunlight, playing hide-and-seek;
Misery and hunger, wait another week!

Great-grandmother Speaks

Pause, child, and stare me in the face
  Before you dare to pass —
Forget the falling shoulder-lace,
  And hear me in the glass!
My pretty mouth you surely know;
  It shouldn't cause dismay —
I am Yourself two lives ago,
  Ten thousand miles away.

My petticoats were just as few,
  My lips were just as red,
I came as lightly home as you,
  And just as late to bed,
All pink above and silk below,
  As bad, as mad, as gay —
But that was ninety years ago,
  Ten thousand miles away.

We didn't sing what RUDY sings
  Nor Mr. CRUMMIT croons,
But simple songs of downright things
  With honest, dancing tunes;
We sang "The Gals of Buffalo",
  "The Thorn" and "Duncan Gray",
But that was ninety years ago,
  Ten thousand miles away.

The polka came, the polka went,
  And who can dance it still,
Or that divine accomplishment,
  The Ginger Blue quadrille?
With portly men on courtly toe
  We ran to meet the day—
But that was ninety years ago,
  Ten thousand miles away.

We'd see the lights of morning break
  And candles burn the wick,
While still a fist was left awake
  To shake a fiddlestick;
And, oh, the fiddle and the bow,
  They didn't beg for pay —
But that was ninety years ago,
  Ten thousand miles away.

And is your heart as light, as light
  As mine was happy then,
Before the gossips learned to write
  With such a spiteful pen,
Before the bitters learned to flow,
  The saxophone to play —
As mine was ninety years ago,
  Ten thousand miles away?

And do you feel the joys we felt
  When Captains held our waist?
I fear those faery pleasures melt
  Before the fox trot's haste;
A rumba on the radio
  Is all you hear today —
And THAT was half-an-hour ago,
  And half-a-mile away!

"THE GIRL" REPLIES:

Great-grandmother, there's no defence
  For half the things I do,
But (pardon the impertinence)
  You weren't so dusty, too;
It's just as well for all, you know,
  The papers never say
What happened ninety years ago,
  Ten thousand miles away!

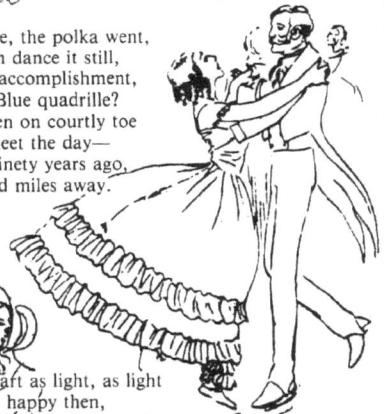

MOVING DAY

When it's Moving Day at midnight,
  And the boarders bolt their doors,
When the watchmen blink and the gunmen wink,
  And the furious landlord snores,
Oh, it's then that we climb from windows
  To take the moon for a ride,
Or fumble and drag at a Gladstone bag
  With a couple of shirts inside.

There's a rope from the second storey,
  There's a phantom hand below,
But little of ghosts who slide down posts
  Does the soul of a landlord know;
Oh, little he thinks of moonlight,
  And little he recks of rent,
But he mutters and moans as he dreams of loans
  At a hundred and five per cent.

All the mugs and jugs go walking,
  All the fruits of bygone debt
We can manage to jam in a broken-down pram
  With a second-hand radio set.
Then hey for the moonlight alleys,
  Yo-ho for the Bourke Street Main!
When janitors yawn in the fogs of dawn,
  They'll bang at our doors in vain.

They'll bang at our doors like thunder
  Ere they woefully find us gone,
And we have no need for a prancing steed
  Or a big pan-
                tech-
                     ni-
                        con,
But we go like the ancient Arabs
  Whenever the mood invites;
We haven't a tent, but we don't pay rent—
  Hooray for Arabian Nights!

The Girl in the Gods

All the din of Donizetti,
    All the singers, high and low,
They are merely there for Betty,
    Upper Circle, second row;
They are merely there to thunder
    (Even Mr. ROSSI nods)
For a girl with eyes of wonder
    In the twilight of the gods.

Like the damsel of Rossetti,
    She is leaning from the sky,
And her name it may be Betty,
    But there's Carmen in her eye.
Boom your mellowest, APOLLO,
    Till the prima donna purrs —
She may grab the flowers that follow,
    But the magic isn't hers.

All the dainty allegrettos,
    Airs that ripple, notes that foam,
Full of passion and stilettos,
    Turning Roseville into Rome,
All the altos and contraltos,
    All the beauty and the pain,
Leave her dreaming in Rialtos
    When she's really in the train.

Then the night is full of daggers
    And a thousand torches glow,
And the Prince of Parma swaggers
    Down the path to "Mon Repos" —
Oh, it's hard to face Artarmon,
    Bricks and mortar, tiles and stones,
When a girl who should be Carmen
    Has to act like Betty Jones!

My Lady's Maid

The girl who stands
  Behind a chair
With prinking hands
  To comb your hair—
Can Age efface
  Without a qualm
So fair a grace
  As this, Madame?

The curls one craves
  Reflected here
(More lasting waves
  Than yours, my dear)
They get no aid,
  They want no skill —
My Lady's Maid
  Adorns them still.

The golden glass
  Floats bright with curls,
Her fingers pass
  Like dancing girls
With crystal dews
  And magic balm,
Not hers to use,
  But YOURS, Madame!

Your flowers and flasks,
  — A.M., P.M.
Her beauty asks
  No help from them.
A Midas paid
  Your modiste's bill?
My Lady's Maid
  Is richer still.

"So slow to-night!
  Not ready yet!"
With icy spite
  You rage and fret;
You fret and rage —
  She keeps her calm.
The pangs of age
  Are yours, Madame!

A fruitless plaint,
  The mirror mocks —
Put back your paint
  And close the box;
Your lips must fade,
  Your flesh grow chill —
My Lady's Maid
  Is younger still!

PASSERS-BY

Dedicated to the girl in the Centre of Australia

What do you see from the window?
  Torrents of runaway feet,
Ribbons and laces, a whirlpool of faces,
  And eyes floating past in the street;
Derricks and dogmen and cranes,
  Traffic that darkens the sky,
Daphne and Doris in somebody's Morris,
  And tramcars and trains
    Passing by.

What do you see from the window?
  Furies of blistering sand;
Endless and level, the plains of the devil
  Where only the camels dare stand.
No one to hear or to speak,
  Telegraph-poles in the sky,
Packhorse and boulders, a skyline that smoulders,
  And teams once a week
    Passing by.

And when I look out of the window,
  Granite and brick fade unseen —
Everything changes to thundering ranges,
  Camels and sand — and Doreen.
Bravely they ride down the years,
  Greeting their God with a cry —
Battered and bleeding, unconquered, unheeding,
  The old pioneers
    Passing by.

WILD GRAPES

The old orchard, full of smoking air,
Full of sour marsh and broken boughs, is there,
But kept no more by vanished Mulligans,
Or Hartigans long drowned in earth themselves,
Who gave this bitter fruit their care.

Here's where the cherries grew that birds forgot,
And apples bright as dogstars; now there is not
An apple or a cherry; only grapes,
But wild ones, Isabella grapes they're called,
Small, pointed, black, like boughs of musket-shot.

Eating their flesh, half-savage with black fur,
Acid and gipsy-sweet, I thought of her,
Isabella, the dead girl, who has lingered on
Mutinously when all have gone away,
In an old orchard where swallows never stir.

Isabella grapes, outlaws of a strange bough,
That in their harsh sweetness remind me somehow,
Of dark hair swinging and silver ear-rings,
A girl half-fierce, half-melting, as these grapes,
Kissed here and killed here —
                    but who remembers now?

24

SILENCE

There aren't any banjos here,
There aren't any occarinas,
There's no riff-raff with a phonograph
Performing on concertinas;
There's only a million gum-trees
And nothing much else to mention,
And trees don't speak more than once a week
And nobody pays attention.

Only the bush by night
With Jupiter shining clear;
You can listen with all your might,
This is all you'll hear —
Silence.

There aren't any mandolins,
You'll never detect harmoniums,
Nor parties in cars, nor steel guitars,
And certainly not euphoniums;
There's only the cold Antarctic,
Penguins and desolation;
The residents muse in their little igloos,
But they don't make conversation.

Only a polar bear,
Only the icebergs round,
Listen as hard as you care,
This is the only sound —
Silence.

There aren't any women here,
They never take tea at eleven,
There's nobody there in the empty chair,
There's nobody humming "Blue Heaven",
There's nobody frying potatoes,
There's nobody making toast,
The laughter's all gone, and the lights aren't on,
And you're standing alone with a ghost.

Only a scent is there still,
Only a note on the wall,
"Forgive me. I've gone with Bill."
What's that in the hall?
Silence.

The GIRL IN THE WINDOW

It's harder than it seems, my dear,
   To catch the smiles you drop;
I've stood here dreaming dreams for hours,
   For hours without a stop.
Your fragrance flutters by,
   A flower in every whiff —
But all you deign to signify
   Is: HIM? Pooh! Sniff!

   You could stun me with a wink,
      you could blind me with a blink,
   You could blow my heart
      to heaven like a bird,
   You could blast me with a "Bah!"
      in your Mousseline-de-soir —
   But what do you say?
         Not a word.

Oh, every time I pass, my dear,
   I lose a night's repose.
I rub against the glass my coarse,
   My coarse, adoring nose.
You turn your pretty face,
   You toss your golden head —
You wouldn't care in any case
   If I dropped dead.

   You could look at me and sneer,
      you could kill me with a jeer,
   You could drag me round
      Australia on a string,
   You could knock a fellow flat
      in your saucy little hat —
   But what do you do?
         Not a thing.

Such frenzy, I confide, my dear,
   With hopeless passion cursed —
You're colder in your pride than snow,
   Than snow in Darlinghurst.
You're prouder than a queen,
   Your silence I adore,
But, oh, your price is plainly seen:
   It's Nine Pounds Four!

   Though you pout at me and mock,
      I could buy your silly frock,
   I could grab you by
      the ankles and elope; ·
   I could purchase with a cheque
      all the sawdust in your neck —
   Could I buy you back to life?
         Not a hope.

26

EVE - OF OTTAWA
A New Dream of Fair Women

"Eve of Ottawa — Empire Delegates Gather." —
"Sydney Morning Herald" headline.

1

I dream of torches that have flickered out,
Of eyes that men have worshipped for a while,
Of lips that toppled kingdoms with a pout,
And built them with a smile.

2

A girl there was whose face was like a flame,
Her mouth a flower, her voice a chime of joy;
"Men saw me, loved, and died. This is my
  name —
HELEN. I come from Troy."

3

And one there was who told of broken years,
Of guns and moonlight, kisses long betrayed,
Some half-remembered girl from
  Armentieres,
Clasping another Maid,

4

That other Mam'selle from an older war,
Girt with a broadsword, blazing in the dark,
Who marched with men five hundred years
  before,
Immortal JOAN of Arc.

5

And one there was who whispered with a
  pang:
"I am that phantom of a minstrel-show,
That LILY of Laguna, whom you sang
And dreamt of long ago."

6

And other ghosts, whose merest dancing smile
Had made a million hearts beat pit-a-pat —
The MAID of Athens, MARY of Argyle,
ELAINE of Astolat,

7

ROSE of Tralee, and ROSE of No Man's
  Land,
TILLY of Bloomsbury, old Drury's NELL,
And SALLY of Our Alley — hand in hand
They passed. Farewell, farewell!

8

And then you came, mysterious, last of all,
Named EVE of Ottawa, a fountain-pen
Perched on one ear, an Empire in your thrall
And fifty million men —

9

And then YOU came, with Hansards in your
  lap
And tariffs like tiaras in your hair,
Bidding us read the news, consult the map
And banish our despair.

10

Who are you, Eve? What apples do you bring?
What happiness, what sorrow? Who can say?
Bound to a new divinity, we sing,
Adams to Eve — ten thousand miles away!

Eating by Yourself

Let aristocratic heroes
   Boast the platters of the Guelph,
You can dream of Trocaderos
   When you're dining by yourself;
You can hover like a glutton,
   You can order what you choose,
Try the fricassee of mutton,
   Toy with terrapin ragouts,
All the claret of Lugano,
   All the fairy teas-and-toasts,
Brought by Ferdinand Romano
   And a staff of lovely ghosts.

First the oysters, round and juicy,
   Served by some delightful girl —
Call her Nancy, call her Lucy,
   She may fetch perhaps a pearl;
Next the soup of tender turtle
   From a nymph with yellow hair —
Call her Mabel, call her Myrtle,
   She can spice it with a stare;
Then the fowl on gleaming china
   That a pretty creature brings —
Call her Dulcie, call her
   Dinah,
You may find a pair
   of wings.

For a moment they will glimmer,
   For a twinkle they will gleam —
Then the kettle starts to simmer
   And they vanish like a dream;
You can whistle for them vainly,
   You may call in tender tones,
But the soup is printed plainly
   With the name of Foggitt, Jones;
Then you suddenly awaken —
   There's a sausage on the shelf,
And the bacon looks like bacon,
   And you're eating by yourself!

THE MOTH & THE CANDLE

O, dear little girl in the Gypsy,
So very disturbingly high,
No doubt you consider them tipsy,
The people you see from the sky.
You frown at the words of a Vandal,
You laugh your contempt of a Goth —
But please to beware of the candle,
O, dear little girl in the Moth,
    Little Girl in the Moth!

You float like a runaway fairy
Where only a fairy could swoop;
It's all so delightfully airy,
A sideslip, a dive, and a loop.
Let Mercury lend you a sandal,
Or Pegasus give you a flight,
But don't go too close to the candle
Like Moths that get burnt in the night,
    Little Girl in the Moth.

We're down in our boots on the level,
You're up in the sky like a speck —
But aeroplanes burn like the devil,
No matter how dainty the wreck.
For danger has torches to dandle
And Moths are too fond of the flame,
And frequently bother a candle
By burning their wings in the same,
    Little Girl in the Moth.

Leave Waghorn the glories of Schneider,
And Hinkler the frenzied Hooray —
A coroner's verdict and rider
Are very dull reading to-day.
The wine that the Jaguars handle
Has funerals under the froth —
So please to take care of the candle,
O, dear little girl in the Moth,
    Little Girl in the Moth!

"LUCKY DOGS"

3

From shop to shop with Marianne,
From side to side they tug,
A Sealyham, a black-and-tan,
A poodle and a pug;
And some are lacquered tooth-and-nail,
And some have scarlet coats,
While like a flail the splendid tail
Of Cochin China floats.

4

The merrier the terriers,
the more they meet and squeak,
Flirtations with Alsatians make
the pavement give a shriek,
But ladies waving handkerchiefs
ignore the little darlings' tiffs —
Surrounded by a sea of sniffs,
they speak
Peke
Peke!

Overture
Oh, where are they tugging them,
why are they hugging them,
What are they lugging them FROM?
A pug and a collie run circles round Polly,
While Pauline goes past with a Pom.

1

Where pink-and-crystal windows burst
With bottled things to eat,
The lucky dogs of Darlinghurst
Go dancing down the street;
Each dainty neck involves a string,
Each string includes a girl —
Two hundred tails in rapture swing,
Two hundred noses curl.

5

And is it merely puppy-love
That moves us in despair
To bend from balconies above
So bitterly to stare?
Alas, our blighted bosoms burst —
Where WE beseech in vain,
The lucky dogs of Darlinghurst
Drag Beauty by a chain!

2

Such quantities of dog-and-girl are going to-and-from,
For Mollie has a collie she can follow with aplomb.
And Poppy has a Pekinese to tangle round her Milanese,
And in and out the pepper-trees, it's Pom
Pom
Pom!

PANTETTE

Pantette, with her little pink trousers
A sort of a silk silhouette,
So Garbo-and-gartery, fire in the artery,
Stopped-for-inspection Pantette —

Pantette has no place in the annals
That echo the deeds of the race,
But who prefers turkey-red flannels
To fringes of unabashed lace?
The kilt still adorns Caledonia,
Pyjamas excite no regret,
And no one considers pneumonia
The logical end of Pantette.

Pantette, so entirely transparent,
A riot of rose and rosette —
Oh, fairy geography, shadow-photography,
Magical-lantern Pantette!

And have we so lightly forgotten
Those garments our grandparents had —
Unthinkable inches of cotton,
Unspeakable objects of plaid?
No longer such heirlooms astonish,
We shudder or smile, and forget,
And nobody tries to admonish
The impudent frills of Pantette.

Pantette, with her pert little ruffles,
Her flutters of cherry georgette,
All pink electricity, pants-and-publicity,
Pooh-to-your-peeping Pantette.

Where ladies in lavender bloomers
Were sold to the devil on bikes,
Pantette is impartial to rumours
And wears what she jolly well likes;
But let her go round as she chooses,
The fact is, we really don't mind,
And nobody's jugular fuses
And no one goes suddenly blind.

Pantette likes the sunlight behind her,
But nobody's died of it yet —
A fig for propriety, into society,
X-ray and all, goes Pantette.

BACKLESS BETTY FROM BONDI

The beach is not entirely free,
The sands are far from trackless,
When Betty dances to the sea,
So rapturously backless;
By this, we don't impute a lack
In one whose back is peerless —

FOR WHO,
POSSESSING SUCH A BACK,
COULD BE DESCRIBED
AS REARLESS?

And, oh, the Euclid of her spine,
The trills, divine and deathless,
That ripple down a magic line
And leave the watcher breathless!
A thousand feet her feet pursue,
With hopeless tread and tireless —

HER BACK IS FULL
OF POOH-FOR-YOU,
HER EYES ARE FULL
OF WIRELESS.

You aldermen who thunder out
Damnation for the Backless,
Your waists, no doubt, are rather stout,
Which makes you somewhat tactless;
And you, arch-bulldogs of the sand,
So big and brown and artless,

WHO PUT THE BELLOW
IN THE BANNED —
INSPECTORS,
DON'T BE HEARTLESS!

Oh, make the great Pacific dry,
And drive the council speechless,
Remove the breakers from Bondi —
The beach, and leave us beachless,
The fair, the bare, the naked-backed,
The beer, the pier, the jetty —

TAKE ANYTHING AT ALL,
IN FACT,
BUT LEAVE,
OH LEAVE US BETTY!

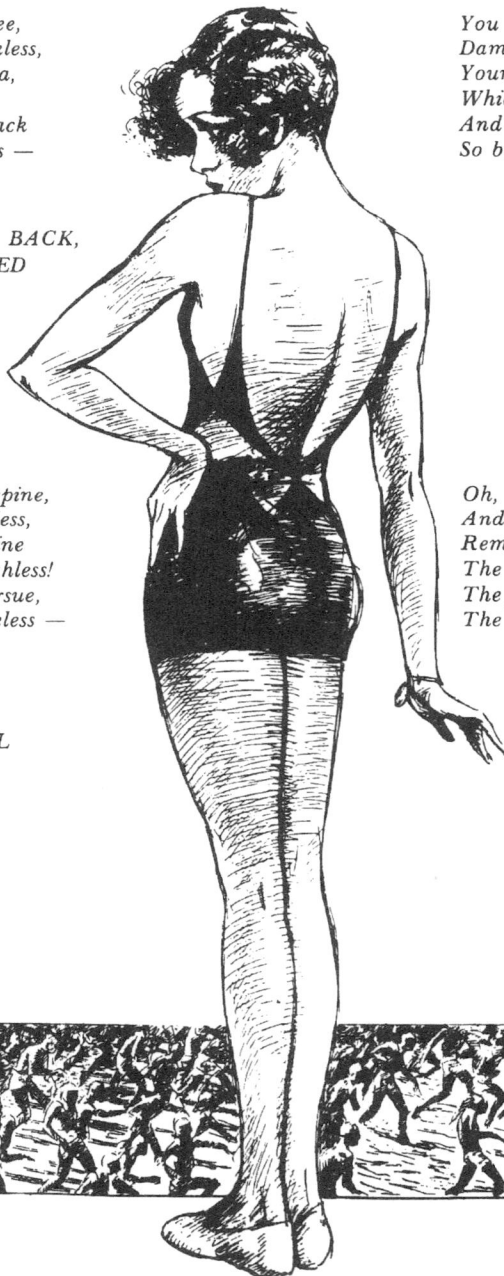

EXTRA HAND

" To cope with the rush of Christmas business, most
of the big city emporiums have put on extra hands . . ."

In the halls of the Ninepenny Bargain,
  In the caves of the great god Cash,
Where the jungle is filled with jargon,
  And the counters are filled with trash,
Where the arc-lights flare and flicker,
  In a storm of string you stand,
With a permanent stack of things to pack,
  An aching wrist and a breaking back,
Little Extra Hand.

In the vaults of the Fourpenny Docket,
  In the teeth of a raving mob,
Where the change comes out of a rocket
  With a hoarse, pneumatic sob,
Like a kind of a kidnapped fairy
  In a strange and sunless land,
You struggle and strap and wrestle and wrap,
  Paper to fold and string to snap,
Little Extra Hand.

Do you hark to the merry gabble
  Or dance to the far-off sound
Of a Christmas that doesn't mean babble
  In a dungeon underground?
But that is a dream of sunshine
  It's harder to understand
When you're doomed to stop in a roaring shop,
  With a pain beneath and an ache on top,
As a little Extra Hand!

Poor Little Rich Girl

Your table is dainty with damask,
You dine upon delicate fare,
And four gold tapers with frosty vapors
Flash in the Dresden ware;

But why do you sit so silent,
And why do you turn so pale,
And why does the ghost of cocoa-and-toast
Trouble your cakes-and-ale?

Your gown is the glory of Lanvin,
Your pearls are a pleasure to see,
Your wine-glass glitters with sherry-and-bitters
Or Pommery '23;

But why do you think of onions,
And why do you sigh for stew
On a plate with a crack in a third-floor-back
Somewhere in Woolloomooloo?

Your fingers are hard with diamonds,
They gleam on a crystal cup;
Their wealth you'd scatter to stand and chatter
Back there — washing up;

But the man who stood at the gas-ring
Belongs to a buried life
And there you are with your caviare,
Poor little rich man's wife!

Darlinghurst Nights

and Morning Glories
Being 47 strange sights
   Observed from eleventh storeys,
In a land of cream puffs and crime,
   By a Flat-roof Professor;
And here set forth in sketch and rhyme

   by

"VIRGIL"
and
KENNETH SLESSOR

ETT IMPRINT, SYDNEY

www.ingramcontent.com/pod-product-compliance
Lightning Source LLC
Chambersburg PA
CBHW060858090426
42737CB00023B/3486